WACKIEST

JOKE

BOOK

THAT'LL
KNOCK-KNOCK
YOU OVER!

Editors of Portable Press

PORTABLE
PRESS

San Diego, California

Portable Press
An imprint of Printers Row Publishing Group
10350 Barnes Canyon Road, Suite 100, San Diego, CA 92121
www.portablepress.com • email: mail@portablepress.com

Printers Row Publishing Group is a division of Readerlink Distribution Services, LLC. Portable Press is a registered trademark of Readerlink Distribution Services, LLC.

The Wackiest Joke Book That'll Knock-Knock You Over! is a compilation of the following two previously published titles: *The Wackiest Joke Book Ever!* and *The Funniest Knock-Knock Jokes Ever!*, © 2017 Portable Press.

All notations of errors or omissions should be addressed to Portable Press, Editorial Department, at the above address.

Publisher: Peter Norton • Associate Publisher: Ana Parker
Publishing/Editorial Team: Vicki Jaeger, Lauren Taniguchi
Editorial Team: JoAnn Padgett, Melinda Allman, Dan Mansfield
Production Team: Jonathan Lopes, Rusty von Dyl

Collected & curated by Kim T. Griswell. Cover & interior concept by Patrick Merrell. Cover & interior by Tanja Fijalkowski.

Library of Congress Cataloging-in-Publication Data available on request.
ISBN: 978-1-68412-278-3

Printed in the United States of America

22 21 20 19 18   2 3 4 5 6

1

FAMILY FUNNIES

Why was the mother firefly unhappy?

Her children weren't very bright.

What does the Pickle family do when their car breaks down?

They dill with it.

Why did the kid leave cheese beside the computer?

To feed the mouse.

Mom: Did you take a shower this morning?

Kid: Why? Is one missing?

Sis: When did you lose your two front teeth?

Bro: I didn't. They're in my pocket.

Who is bigger, Mrs. Bigger or her baby?

Her baby is a little Bigger.

FAMILY FUNNIES

Dad: Why did you fail your history test?

Kid: All the questions were about things that happened before I was born.

Mama Giraffe: Eat your leaves, son. They put color in your cheeks.

Giraffe Son: Who wants green cheeks?

Why wasn't Mom worried about the moose in the kitchen?

It was a chocolate mousse.

Elephant Baby: Pops, do elephants really have good memories?

Elephant Dad: I forget.

If you eat one half of an apple pie and
your sister eats the other half,
what are you left with?

A very angry mom.

Why did Ed's parents name their
second son Ed, too?

Because two Eds are better than one.

Bro: I just spotted a leopard!

Sis: Don't be silly. Leopards
are born that way.

Why don't dads ever buy
new underwear?

Because *under*wear never gets worn *out*.

FAMILY FUNNIES

Grandma: I once typed an essay on the belly of a frog.

Grandkid: Wow! How'd you get the frog into the typewriter?

What's the best cure for sleepwalking?

Put tacks on the floor.

Dad: Why did you dip your computer in melted caramel?

Kid: I wanted a candied Apple.

How can you tell a baby snake?

By its rattle.

FAMILY FUNNIES

Why did Grandpa's hair turn gray
before his moustache?

It was older.

Mom: I found a restaurant where
we can eat dirt cheap!

Dad: I'd rather eat steak.

Who isn't your sister or brother but
is still a child of your parents?

You.

What did the mama cow say
to her calf?

"Go to sleep! It's pasture bedtime."

FAMILY FUNNIES

Hey! There's a family of horses moving in next door!

Great! They'll make good nei-ei-ei-ghbors.

How many paws does a lion have?

One Paw. Just like everyone else.

What happened when the baby drank 8 colas?

He burped 7-Up.

Dad: Why are you eating your homework?

Kid: The teacher said it was a piece of cake.

What happened when Mom put too much mousse in her hair?

She grew antlers.

Why was the kid late to school every day?

The teacher said it was never too late to learn.

What's worse than a crying baby?

Two crying babies.

What did the mirror say to the dresser?

"I see your drawers!"

FAMILY FUNNIES

Why did Farmer John borrow a needle from his wife?

He couldn't find the one in the haystack.

Why did the kid put the cake in the freezer?

It needed icing.

Kid: How many apples grow on a tree?

Mom: All of them.

Do you have to be royal to ride in a carriage?

Not if you're a baby.

Which family member is purple?

Your grape-grandmother.

Kid: Dad, which board do you need to finish the fence?

Dad: The last one.

Which relatives always come to family picnics?

The ants.

Which grade should you never get on a report card?

D. It makes Ma mad.

What is big and yellow and comes in the morning to brighten Mom's day?

The school bus.

Why did Dad work late at the pajama factory?

He was on the nightie shift.

Kid: What's the best way to avoid wrinkles?

Grandma: Don't sleep in your clothes.

Kid: Will the pancakes be long? I'm starving.

Dad: No. They'll be round.

What do you call rotten eggs, spoiled milk, and moldy bread?

Gross-eries.

Mom: How do you know the dog ate your homework?

Kid: I fed it to him.

What do you give a sick female relative?

Auntie-biotics.

Grandpa: I've been swimming since I was five years old.

Grandkid: You must be really tired.

2

ANIMAL SILLIES

What do whales chew?

Blubber gum.

What is black and white and green and black and white?

Two zebras fighting over a pickle.

What kind of animal lives in a can?

A cantaloupe.

Why did the elephant quit the circus?

He was tired of working for peanuts.

Who wrote *The Worst Joke Book Ever*?

Terry Bull.

What is white on the top, yellow in the middle, and white on the bottom?

A lion sandwich.

ANIMAL SILLIES

**What is black and white and red
all over?**

A zebra hiding in a bottle of ketchup.

How are playing cards like wolves?

They both travel in packs.

**What one-horned animal won't take
"no" for an answer?**

The why-nocerous.

Why do giraffes have such long necks?

Because their feet stink.

ANIMAL SILLIES

Why did the watchdog sleep all the time?

His owner forgot to wind him.

Why are there no aardvarks in Alaska?

They can't afford the plane fare.

What was the silly chicken doing in the garden?

Sitting on an eggplant.

What do you call a dog that sneezes?

A germy shepherd.

ANIMAL SILLIES

What do you call a bunny that gives out parking tickets?

Meter Rabbit.

Why wouldn't the horse talk to the cow?

Everything she said was udder nonsense.

Where do cows go on vacation?

Moo York.

Why did the hippo sit on a pumpkin?

He wanted to play squash.

ANIMAL SILLIES

What do baby bunnies learn in school?

The alfalfa-bet.

What's the difference between a platypus and a peanut butter sandwich?

A platypus doesn't stick to the roof of your mouth.

Why do squirrels live in trees?

To avoid all the nuts on the ground.

How do dogs keep up on local news?

Smellovision.

ANIMAL SILLIES

How does a polite lion greet a hunter?

"Pleased to eat you!"

What is the biggest ant?

The elephant!

Which animal never remembers names?

The owl. It's always saying,
"Who? Who?"

What's the best use of cowhide?

To keep the cow together.

ANIMAL SILLIES

How do you know there's an elephant in your sandwich?

It's too heavy to lift.

How do fish buy things online?

With a credit cod.

Which bird is always out of breath?

A puffin.

Why did the dog go to jail?

He didn't pay his barking ticket.

ANIMAL SILLIES

Why do rabbits have fur coats?

Because they'd look silly in
leather jackets.

**Why don't polar bears live in
the desert?**

They can't bear the heat.

How many kinds of gnus are there?

Two. Good gnus and bad gnus.

**What do you call an elephant in
a phone booth?**

Stuck.

ANIMAL SILLIES

How can you keep milk from spoiling?

Leave it in the cow.

How can you tell which end of
a worm is its head?

Tickle it in the middle and see which
end laughs.

What do you get if you cross a barber
with a sheep?

A baa-aa-aad haircut.

How do you get fur from a bear?

Run as fast as you can!

ANIMAL SILLIES

Why did the ram fall off the cliff?

It didn't see the ewe turn.

What is a skunk's favorite sandwich?

Peanut butter and smelly.

Why did the cow stop giving milk?

She wasn't in the moooooo-d.

What do you call a canine magician?

A labracadabrador.

ANIMAL SILLIES

Why do ducks make the best detectives?

They always quack the case.

What did the nearsighted porcupine say to the cactus?

"Hi, Mom!"

What do alligators call children?

Appetizers.

What do dogs eat at the movies?

Pupcorn.

3

SILLYSAURUS

What kind of dinosaur wears
a cowboy hat and boots?

Tyrannosaurus tex.

Why did the raptor paint its
claws yellow?

So it could hide in the banana tree.

What goes *thump*, *squish*,
thump, *squish*?

A T. rex with one wet sneaker.

Which dinosaur
has the biggest vocabulary?

A Thesaurus.

What is a dinosaur's favorite snack?

Macaroni and trees.

Which dinosaur demolishes buildings?

Tyrannosaurus wrecks.

**What do you call a dinosaur
that stubs its toe?**

Sore-toe-a-saurus.

**Did you hear the one about
the pterodactyl egg?**

It was a very old yolk.

**Why did the plesiosaur eat a fleet of
ships carrying potatoes?**

Because no one can eat just one
potato ship.

**What do you get when you cross
a dinosaur and a wizard?**

Tyrannosaurus hex.

SILLYSAURUS

What was the world's fastest dinosaur?

The prontosaurus.

How do you tell a dinosaur to hurry?

"Shake a leg-osaurus!"

Why are dinosaurs big, green, and scaly?

If they were small, yellow, and fuzzy, they would be tennis balls.

Why did the stegosaurus climb a tree?

Because the sign said KEEP OFF THE GRASS.

What is T. rex's favorite game?

Swallow the leader.

Why did the pterodactyl cross the road?

Because there weren't any chickens yet.

**Why shouldn't you teach T. rex
to add 4 + 4?**

You might get 8 (ate).

**Which dinosaur keeps you
awake at night?**

The bronto-snore-us.

What follows a stegosaurus
wherever it goes?

Its tail.

What do you get if you give
a dinosaur a pogo stick?

Big holes in your driveway.

What do you call the king of the
dinosaurs after it evolves into a chicken?

Tyrannosaurus pecks.

Why did the sauropod wear
purple pajamas?

Because its pink ones were
in the wash.

What kind of dinosaur has no wings, but flies all over?

The kind that needs a bath.

How do you get down from a dinosaur?

You don't! You get down from a goose.

What time is it when a dinosaur sits on your toilet?

Time to get a new toilet.

Which dinosaur was a crybaby?

Tear-annosaurus rex.

**What do you do
with a yellow triceratops?**

Teach it to be brave.

**What was the brontosaurus's
favorite game?**

Squash.

What does a triceratops sit on?

Its tricera-bottom.

Why did T. rex cross the road?

To eat the chickens on the other side.

What do you call a polite dinosaur?

A please-iosaur.

**Why are dinosaurs always found
in the ground?**

Because they couldn't climb trees.

Which dinosaur caught the worm?

Archaeopteryx. It was an early bird.

**What kind of dinosaurs live
in graveyards?**

Cemetery-dactyls.

SILLYSAURUS

Why do museums have so many old dinosaur bones?

They can't find any new ones.

Why did the dinosaur eat a cow and three ducks?

It liked milk and quackers.

What do you do when a dinosaur breaks its toe?

Call a very big toe truck.

What do you call a T. rex having a temper tantrum?

Brat-T rex.

SILLYSAURUS

Why invite a dinosaur to your birthday party?

They're tons of fun.

Why did dinosaurs become extinct?

They didn't want to hear any more dinosaur jokes.

Where was the dinosaur when the sun went down?

In the dark.

Why did the apatosaurus devour the factory?

She was a plant eater.

SILLYSAURUS

Which dinosaurs make the best police officers?

Tricera-cops.

When is a dinosaur likely to enter your house?

When the door is open.

What's bright blue and weighs 2,000 pounds?

A dinosaur holding its breath.

How long were a velociraptor's legs?

Long enough to reach the ground.

4

ODDBALLS

How do you make a hot dog stand?

Steal its chair.

What is the first thing a ball does when it stops rolling?

It looks round.

ODDBALLS

What do you call a six-foot-tall basketball player?

Shortie.

What is stranger than seeing a catfish?

Seeing a goldfish bowl.

What can you serve but never eat?

A tennis ball.

Why are baseball games played at night?

Because bats sleep during the day.

ODDBALLS

What's the bounciest room in a palace?

The ballroom.

Why did the umpire throw the chicken out of the game?

He suspected fowl play.

Why can't pigs play basketball?

They hog the ball.

What are the last words of "The Star Spangled Banner"?

Play ball!

Why are fish lousy at volleyball?

They run away from the net.

**What is harder to catch
the faster you run?**

Your breath.

**What does an umpire always do
before he eats?**

Brushes off the plate.

**Soccer player: I could kick
myself for missing that goal.**

Teammate: Don't bother.
You'll probably miss.

**What did the batter say when
the coach called in a new pitcher?**

"That's a relief!"

**How is a baseball catcher
like a farmer?**

They both chase fowls.

Why are basketballs always wet?

The players dribble a lot.

Why do golfers like to eat Cheerios?

Because there's a hole in every one.

ODDBALLS

How are football players like pilots?

They both make touchdowns.

**What's the difference between
a bad goalie and Cinderella?**

Cinderella got to the ball.

Mom: Which player is the fullback?

Kid: The one who ate too much
before the game.

**Which three letters will stop
a quarterback sneak?**

I-C-U!

ODDBALLS

What bird can be found at the end of every race?

The puffin.

What did the dog say when a ball landed on top of the house?

"Roof! Roof!"

How do you keep squirrels off the football field?

Hide the ball. It drives them nuts!

Which sport is the quietest?

Bowling. You can hear a pin drop.

Wide receiver: What's the best way to catch a ball?

Coach: Have someone throw it to you.

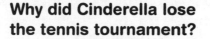

Why did Cinderella lose the tennis tournament?

She had a pumpkin for a coach.

When do baseball players wear armor?

For knight games.

Golfer: Golf is a funny game.

Caddy: It's not supposed to be.

What is a basketball player's favorite kind of story?

Tall tales.

What's the funniest baseball team?

The New York Prankees.

What do you call a girl who stands in the middle of a volleyball court?

Annette.

Coach: You'd be better at bowling than baseball.

Kid: Why?

Coach: You always get strikes!

Why did the football fan go to the bathroom?

He wanted to watch the Toilet Bowl.

What's a basketball player's favorite snack?

Cookies, because they can dunk them.

Why did the baseball player keep winking?

He needed batting practice.

Why did the chicken cross the baseball field?

The umpire called a fowl.

Sports stories:

Extra Innings by Willy Win,
illustrated by Betty Wont

What has 18 legs and catches flies?

A baseball team.

Where do old bowling balls end up?

In the gutter.

**How do hens root for their favorite
football team?**

They egg them on.

ODDBALLS

Why did the shortstop get arrested?

He was caught stealing third base.

**Why do porcupines win
every ball game?**

They have the most points.

5

THAT'S HISTORICAL!

Who was America's funniest
Founding Father?

Benjamin Pranklin.

Where was
Queen Elizabeth II crowned?

On her head.

THAT'S HISTORICAL!

Teacher: For tonight's homework, write an essay on Abraham Lincoln.

Student: I'd rather write on paper.

Who was France's sleepiest emperor?

Nap-oleon.

Which American president wore the biggest shoes?

The one with the biggest feet.

Which Egyptian queen loved spaghetti?

Cleo-pasta.

How was Thomas Jefferson like a fish?

He was a flounder of his country.

Why did Paul Revere always carry a handkerchief?

He was the town crier.

Why was Queen Elizabeth I buried at Westminster Abbey?

Because she was dead.

Which patriotic song comes in handy when you sneeze?

Hanky Doodle Dandy.

THAT'S HISTORICAL!

What did Pocahontas become on her 21st birthday?

A year older.

Who invented the first airplane that didn't fly?

The Wrong brothers.

Who was purple and conquered the world?

Alexander the Grape.

Where is Timbuktu?

Between Timbuk-one and Timbuk-three.

Why did Teddy Roosevelt throw away his sleeping bag?

He couldn't get it to wake up.

Which president was the best social-networker?

Abraham LinkedIn.

How were the Pilgrims like ants?

They lived in colonies.

Which famous French landmark can't stand up?

The Eiffel (I fell) Tower.

What's the smelliest statue in Egypt?

The Stynx.

Which Leonardo da Vinci painting won't stop complaining?

The Moaning Lisa.

What did Benjamin Franklin say when he discovered electricity?

Nothing. He was too shocked.

Why didn't the lookout on the *Titanic* spot the iceberg?

He had bad ice-sight.

Which telephone inventor had a cookie named after him?

Alexander Graham Cracker.

Which Roman emperor always had a cold?

Julius Sneezer.

Who was the world's smartest pig?

Ein-swine.

What part of London is in China?

The letter "n."

If Genghis Khan were alive today,
what would he be most famous for?

His age.

How did George Washington
cross the Delaware?

In a boat.

Where can you find Moscow?

In the barn, next to Pa's cow.

What do Alexander the Great and
Winnie the Pooh have in common?

Their middle name.

How often do ships like
the *Titanic* sink?

Just once.

Two wrongs don't make a right, so
what do two rights make?

An airplane.

What did Sir Lancelot wear to bed?

A knight gown.

Which soldiers traveled the most?

The Romans.

How is the United States like
a healthy kid?

Both have good constitutions.

Why was Billy the Kid sitting on
his mother's stove?

He wanted to be home on the range.

Where was the Treaty of 1783 signed?

At the bottom.

What happened when an apple hit
Sir Isaac Newton on the head?

He realized the gravity of the situation.

THAT'S HISTORICAL!

Why don't you ever hear about Betsy Ross?

Interest in her has flagged.

Is the capital of Missouri pronounced Saint Loo-is or Saint Loo-ey?

Neither. It's pronounced Jefferson City.

How do we know the ancient Romans were smart?

They understood Latin.

What's the capital of Pennsylvania?

P.

How would a robber get gold out
of Fort Knox?

Through the door.

What was the closest thing to
King George III?

His underwear.

What happened to the inventor
of sandpaper?

He had a rough time.

What stands in New York harbor
and sneezes all day?

The Achoo of Liberty.

6

TOAD-ALLY WACKY

What is green and red all over?

A frog holding its breath.

Why couldn't the lizard stop singing?

He was a rap-tile.

What's green and bumpy and jumps a lot?

A cucumber with hiccups.

How do you catch a baby frog?

With a toad-pole.

How is a toad like a brick?

Neither one can play the trumpet.

What kind of lizard tells jokes?

A stand-up chameleon.

Why did the frog think it was a bird?

Because it was pigeon-toad.

What do you get when you cross a turtle with a sheep?

A turtle-neck sweater.

How many witches does it take to change a lightbulb?

One...but she changes it into a toad!

Diner: Waiter! Why is there a frog in my soup?

Waiter: Looks like it's eating the fly.

What do frogs always catch during baseball games?

Pop flies.

What do you get when you cross a toad with a pig?

A wart-hog.

What did the toad say to the kangaroo?

"I feel kinda jumpy today.
How about you?"

What happens when you throw a toad into the ocean?

It gets toad-ally wet.

What do turtles do on their birthday?

Shellabrate!

What do you say if you meet a toad?

"Wart's new?"

What kind of frog can be found at the North Pole?

One that's toad-ally lost.

Why did the toad sit on a marshmallow?

So it wouldn't fall into the hot chocolate.

What's the funniest place in the frog pond?

The silly pad.

What do you get when you cross a toad with Luke Skywalker?

Star Warts.

Why can't you believe anything toads tell you?

They're am-*fib*-ians.

How do you get a frog to fly?

Buy it an airplane ticket.

TOAD-ALLY WACKY

What kind of slippers did
Frogerella wear to the ball?

Open-toad.

What goes *ribbit, ribbit, thunk*?

A frog laughing its head off.

Why did the frog jump over the moon?

Because the cow was on vacation.

What did the frog say when
it couldn't stop coughing?

"Sorry, I have a person in my throat."

TOAD-ALLY WACKY

What's green and warty and goes up
and down all day?

A toad in an elevator.

What happens if you swallow a toad?

You croak!

Why did the frog take the bus?

Its car got toad.

Where do toads hang their coats?

In the croakroom.

**What do you get if you cross
a toad with a crocodile?**

Leaping lizards.

**What goes
dit-dit-dot-croak, dit-dit-dot-croak?**

Morse toad.

**What's the best way to catch
a tadpole?**

Have someone throw it at you.

**Why did the boy put a mouse in
his sister's bed?**

He couldn't catch a toad.

What do you get when you cross an alligator with a pickle?

A croco-dill.

What do toads drink in winter?

Hot croako.

7

THAT'S BANANAS!

Why did the elephant stomp on the banana?

He wanted a banana splat!

Why aren't bananas lonely?

They always travel in bunches.

THAT'S BANANAS!

What is King Kong's favorite musical?

Little Orphan Banannie.

How do monkeys get downstairs?

They slide down the banana-ster.

**Why didn't the monkey undress
for its bath?**

Because it was wearing a bathrobe.

**What's a monkey's
favorite ice cream?**

Chocolate chimp.

THAT'S BANANAS!

Which side of a monkey has the most fur?

The outside.

What is long and yellow and always points north?

A magnetic banana.

Which monkeys can fly?

Hot-air baboons.

Why couldn't the monkey open the piano?

The keys were inside.

THAT'S BANANAS!

What is yellow and wears a mask?

The Lone Banana.

**What did the monkey say to
the sleeping banana?**

"Stop snoring before you wake up
the whole bunch."

**Moviegoer: I can't believe how much
your monkey liked that movie.**

Lady with monkey: I can't either!
He hated the book.

Why don't chimpanzees have tails?

So they won't get caught in
revolving doors.

THAT'S BANANAS!

What's yellow and writes?

A ballpoint banana.

**What do you call a monkey whose
bananas were stolen?**

Furious George.

What is yellow and goes up and down?

A banana in an elevator.

**What kind of monkeys live at
the North Pole?**

Cold ones.

THAT'S BANANAS!

Why do monkeys have fur?

So their underwear won't show.

**What did the banana say to
the monkey?**

Don't be silly—bananas can't talk!

**What do you call two monkeys
who hang over a window?**

Kurt-n-Rod.

**How do you keep a monkey from going
through the eye of a needle?**

Tie a knot in its tail.

THAT'S BANANAS!

Why did the monkey put banana peels on his feet?

He needed a new pair of slippers.

What do you call a monkey that swims with crocodiles?

Dinner.

What's yellow and hairy?

A banana wearing a toupee.

What should you do if you find ten little monkeys sleeping on your bed?

Get a hotel room.

THAT'S BANANAS!

Why did the monkey try to eat its bicycle?

It had a banana seat.

Where do you find monkeys?

Depends on where you left them.

What do you call a 2,000-pound gorilla?

Sir.

Why did the monkey close its eyes when it looked in the mirror?

To see how it looked when it was asleep.

What lives in a vineyard and swings through the vines?

Tarzan of the Grapes.

How long should a monkey's legs be?

Long enough to reach the ground.

Why did the banana go out with a prune?

Because it couldn't get a date.

Why did the banana cross the road?

It was running away from the monkey.

THAT'S BANANAS!

Traci: Why do elephants paint their faces yellow?
Stacy: I don't know, why?
Traci: So they can hide in banana trees.
Stacy: That's silly! I've never seen an elephant in a banana tree.
Traci: See! It works!

What do you call a banana with wings?

A fruit fly.

What's the opposite of a gorilla?

A stop-rilla.

8

SPACE CADETS

What do you get when you cross an alien with a hot drink?

Gravi-tea.

Astronaut: Captain, we're going faster than the speed of sound.

Captain: What did you say?

Why should you never insult a Martian?

It might get its feelers hurt.

What's the center of gravity?

The letter "v."

What do you do with a green alien?

Wait until he ripens.

Why didn't Little Bo Peep fly to Mars?

She couldn't find her space-sheep.

What did the mouse pilot say to the shuttle passengers?

"This is your captain squeaking!"

If Martians live on Mars and Venusians live on Venus, what lives on Pluto?

Fleas!

Where do astronauts get their degrees?

From a mooniversity.

Favorite do-it-yourself book:

Space Travel by Bill Jerome Rocket

How do you tie your shoes
in outer space?

With an astro-knot.

Which planet has the most cows?

The mooooon.

Why did the shuttle pilot refuse
to take flying lessons?

It was a crash course.

Why did the astronaut let go
of her sundae?

She wanted an ice-cream float.

Where do you find black holes?

In black socks.

Why can't astronauts keep jobs?

They always get fired after training.

What do you get when you cross a chicken with an alien?

An eggstra-terrestrial.

What is a Jedi's favorite snack?

Obi-Wan Cannoli.

SPACE CADETS

Why don't aliens celebrate birthdays?

They don't want to give away
their presence.

**What did the astronaut say when she
walked into the space shuttle?**

"Ouch!"

How many letters are in the alphabet?

Twenty-four...because E.T. went home.

Why haven't astronauts visited Mars?

They haven't been invited.

**What do the planets get
after orbiting the sun all day?**

Dizzy.

How do you wash a space shuttle?

Fly it through a meteor shower.

Favorite tabloid tale:

I Saw an Alien by Omar Goodness

Why did the alien abduct a dachshund?

It wanted a down-to-Earth pet.

Besides shooting stars, which other stars have tails?

Dory, Tigger, and Bambi.

What do you call a wizard in space?

A flying sorcerer.

What do you call a robot that takes the longest route?

R2-Detour.

What is fast, loud, and crunchy?

A rocket chip.

DON'T BEE SILLY!

Why do bees hum?

Because they don't know how to whistle.

Can bees fly in rain?

Only if they wear their yellow jackets.

DON'T BEE SILLY!

Why don't bees play baseball?

They're always too bees-y.

Why do bees walk on the ceiling?

If they walked on the floor,
someone might step on them.

**Doctor, Doctor! I keep seeing bees
circling my head!**

Don't worry. It's just a bug that's
going around.

**What's black and yellow and goes *zzub,
zzub*?**

A bee flying backward.

DON'T BEE SILLY!

Why is the letter "A" like a flower?

Because a bee always comes after it.

How do you know bees are happy?

They hum while they work.

Why do bees have sticky hair?

Because they use honeycombs.

**What did the bee order at
the fast-food joint?**

A hum-burger.

DON'T BEE SILLY!

Who's a bee's favorite composer?

Bee-thoven.

What did the bee in the sauna say?

"'Swarm in here!"

What was the bee's favorite musical?

Stinging in the Rain.

What is a bee's favorite sport?

Rug-bee.

DON'T BEE SILLY!

Book buzz:

Looking at Bees by Amos Skeeto

What do you get when you cross
a skunk with a bee?

You get stung by a stinker.

What do you call a wasp?

A wanna-bee.

Where do you take a wasp
with a broken wing?

The waspital.

DON'T BEE SILLY!

How do bees get to school?

They take the buzz.

**What do you call a bee having
a bad hair day?**

A frizz-bee.

What comes after an April bee?

A May-bee.

**What's black and yellow and
flies above the clouds?**

A bee in an airplane.

DON'T BEE SILLY!

What's worse than being a fool?

Fooling with a bee!

What kind of wasp can you wear?

A yellow jacket.

Who writes books for little bees?

Bee-trix Potter.

What buzzes and is wanted by the FBI?

A killer bee.

DON'T BEE SILLY!

How does a bee cut firewood?

With a buzz saw.

**What do you get when you cross
a sheep with a bee?**

A baaaa-humbug.

Girl: I'd like to buy a bee.

Pet store owner: We don't sell bees.

**Girl: Then why do you have one in
your front window?**

Which insect can't play football?

The fumble-bee.

DON'T BEE SILLY!

What kind of suit does a bee
wear to work?

A buzz-ness suit.

Why did the bee go to the doctor?

It had hives.

What did the rose say to the bee?

"Buzz off!"

Which insect gets the best grade
in English?

The spelling bee.

DON'T BEE SILLY!

What does a bee sit on?

Its bee-hind.

What did the robber say to the bee?

"Your honey or your life."

What kind of phones do bees use?

Cell phones.

Where do bees go on vacation?

Stingapore.

10

SCARED SILLY

What happened when the werewolf swallowed the clock?

He got ticks.

Why wouldn't the vampire climb into his coffin at sunrise?

He was an all-day sucker.

**What are a zombie's least
favorite letters?**

D K (decay).

**Where does Medusa go when
she visits Arizona?**

The Petrified Forest.

Why won't Bigfoot cross the road?

Because that's what chickens do.

**Do mummies like to visit
King Tut's tomb?**

Naw...they wouldn't be caught
dead there.

**Who's the best dancer at
the monster ball?**

The Boogieman.

**What did one zombie say to
the other zombie?**

"Get a life!"

**What does the Loch Ness monster
eat for breakfast?**

Bagels and lochs.

Why do vampire bats use red markers?

They like to draw blood.

**What kind of monster is never around
when you need him?**

A wherewolf.

Where do mummies go for pizza?

Pizza Tut.

Why didn't the zombie lose its teeth?

It used toothpaste.

**Why did King Kong climb
the Empire State Building so quickly?**

He had a plane to catch.

Which artist has the most haunted paintings?

Vincent van Ghost.

How many vampires does it take to change a lightbulb?

None. They prefer the dark.

What kind of key opens a casket?

A skeleton key.

Why did Batman go to the pet store?

To buy a Robin.

How does Dracula like his coffee?

De-coffin-ated.

**Which three letters terrify
the Invisible Man?**

I-C-U.

**What does Frankenstein do
first thing every morning?**

He wakes up.

**Why does Bigfoot always leave
behind footprints?**

Because they're dirty.

Why do dragons love knights?

Because they're crunchy and good
with ketchup.

**What do you call two witches
who share an apartment?**

Broom-mates.

**What did the mommy ghost say
to the baby ghost?**

"Don't spook until you're spooken to."

**How did the zombie feel after
partying all night?**

Dead on his feet.

SCARED SILLY

What is King Kong's favorite sandwich?

Go-rilla cheese.

How does a witch tell time?

With a witch watch.

Why doesn't the mummy take a vacation?

Because if he relaxes too much, he'll unwind.

Why did Dracula run around his coffin?

To catch up on his sleep.

Where do ghosts like to swim?

The Dead Sea.

What was the pirate's favorite fish?

The swordfish.

Where do vampires keep their money?

In blood banks.

**How could the mummy have
a brother if the mummy's brother
had no brothers?**

The mummy is a woman.

SCARED SILLY

Why did the wolfman scratch himself?

No one else knew where he itched.

Why didn't the skeleton kid like
to go to school?

Her heart wasn't in it.

When is it bad luck to have
a black cat cross your path?

When you're a mouse.

How did the Phantom of the Opera
get out of a locked room?

He played the piano until he found
the right key.

SCARED SILLY

What is Dracula's favorite fast food?

Fangfurters.

**What has two arms, two wings,
three heads, and eight legs?**

A man riding a horse holding a chicken.

**Where did the Headless Horseman
find his head?**

In the last place he looked.

Who's the clumsiest monster?

Clodzilla.

Why was the photographer arrested?

Because he shot people and then
blew them up.

**Why did Godzilla wrap a long string
around a Japanese city?**

He wanted a Tokyo-yo.

**Why do zombies dine
at the fanciest restaurants?**

They only eat gore-met food.

Is Ghostland a country?

No. It's a terror-tory.

SCARED SILLY

Why did Bigfoot Jr. shave off all his hair?

He wanted to be a little bare (bear).

**What's the first thing ghosts do
when they get into a car?**

They boo-ckle up.

What is a sea monster's favorite lunch?

A submarine sandwich.

Why do witches fly on broomsticks?

They're too lazy to walk.

What do you call a zombie track team?

The Running Dead.

What's a cannibal's favorite pizza?

Cheese, with everyone on it.

What is sweet, brown, and deadly?

Shark-infested chocolate pudding.

What was the baby zombie's favorite toy?

Its heady bear.

11

EXTRA WACKY

Why couldn't Cinderella go to
King Neptune's ball?

She didn't have a ferry godmother.

What is round and has a bad temper?

A vicious circle.

**What should you do if you break
your arm in two places?**

Stay away from those places.

What is Tigger's favorite hot dog?

Wienie the Pooh.

**Patient: My ear's ringing. What
should I do?**

Doctor: Answer it.

What is a pig's favorite fairy tale?

Slopping Beauty.

Which animals are best at multiplication?

Rabbits.

What happened when the king's men told Humpty Dumpty a joke?

He fell for it.

Teacher: What is 5Q + 5Q?

Student: 10Q.

Teacher: You're welcome!

Painful reading:

The Patient with the Exploding Bottom
by Stan Wellback

**What do you call a boomerang that
doesn't come back to you?**

A bummerang.

**How many skunks does it take
to make a big stink?**

A phew.

Why is lava red and hot?

Because if it were white and cold,
it would be snow.

Did you know it takes three sheep to make one sweater?

I didn't even know they could knit!

What speaks every language?

An echo.

What do you get if you cross a dog with a chicken?

A pooched egg.

What did the skunk say when the wind changed?

"It all comes back to me now."

EXTRA WACKY

Why are barns so noisy?

The cows have horns.

Rooster #1 laid 3 eggs.
Rooster #2 laid 4 eggs.
How many eggs do you have?

None. Roosters don't lay eggs.

What do you call a small billy goat?

A peanut butter.

Where can you find an ocean
with no water?

On a map.

When is a worm safe from the early bird?

When it sleeps late.

What is 11 + 2 + 4 - 17?

A lot of work for nothing!

What do you call a boy with a car on his head?

Jack.

Patient: Doctor, Doctor! My nose is running.

Doctor: No. I think it's not.

**Did you hear about
the clothesline robbery?**

The underwear was held up by
two clothespins.

**What do you call
a three-footed aardvark?**

A yard-vark.

**What did the bear cub say when
his friend came to visit?**

"I'd like you to meet my den mother."

Why did Miss Muffet need a map?

Because she lost her whey.

What kind of paper makes the best kites?

Flypaper.

Zach: Josh is whispering in class.

Teacher: Why does that bother you?

Zach: I can't hear what he's saying.

Why did Captain Hook cross the road?

To get to the secondhand shop.

What do you call a tuba's father?

Ooom-papa.

How many bugs can you put in an empty pint jar?

One. After that, it's not empty.

What's the best brain food?

Noodle soup.

Why did the math teacher skip the chapter on circles?

They were pointless.

What happened when 19 and 20 got into a fight?

Twenty-won.

**What makes kindergarten teachers
so good?**

They know how to make
the little things count.

**What sits on the ocean bottom
and shakes?**

A nervous wreck.

What's green and goes camping?

A brussels scout.

Stinkiest book:

Too Many Beans by Wynn D. Bottom

What's pink and fluffy?

Pink fluff.

What's blue and pink and fluffy?

Pink fluff holding its breath.

**What did one potato chip
say to the other?**

"Let's go for a dip!"

How do little shellfish travel?

By taxi crab.

Why did the driver hold his nose?

His car had gas.

What kind of pliers do you use in math?

Multipliers.

How much dirt is in a hole with
a three-foot circumference?

None. Holes are empty.

Which cowboy lives in the ocean?

Billy the Squid.

12

KNOCK-NAMES

Knock-knock!

Who's there?
Doris.
Doris who?
Doris open. Can I come in?

KNOCK-NAMES

Knock-knock!
Who's there?
Fanny.
Fanny who?
Fanny-body knocks, I'm not home.

Knock-knock!
Who's there?
Athena.
Athena who?
Athena flying saucer!

Knock-knock!
Who's there?
Emerson.
Emerson who?
Emerson nice sneakers you're wearing.

KNOCK-NAMES

Knock-knock!
Who's there?
Hannah.
Hannah who?
Hannah partridge in a pear tree.

Knock-knock!
Who's there?
Sancho.
Sancho who?
Sancho an email but you never answered.

Knock-knock!
Who's there?
Lionel.
Lionel who?
Lionel bite you if you stick your head in its mouth.

Knock-knock!
Who's there?
Howell.
Howell who?
Howell you find out if you don't open the door?

Knock-knock!
Who's there?
José.
José who?
José can you see...

Knock-knock!
Who's there?
Kent.
Kent who?
Kent you see for yourself?

KNOCK-NAMES

Knock-knock!
Who's there?
Gus.
Gus who?
That's what *you're* supposed to do!

Knock-knock!
Who's there?
Eliza.
Eliza who?
Eliza lot so don't trust 'im.

Knock-knock!
Who's there?
Carmen.
Carmen who?
Carmen get it!

KNOCK-NAMES

Knock-knock!
Who's there?
Howard.
Howard who?
Howard I know?

Knock-knock!
Who's there?
Freddy.
Freddy who?
Freddy or not, here I come!

Knock-knock!
Who's there?
Celeste.
Celeste who?
Celeste time I knock on *your* door.

KNOCK-NAMES

Knock-knock!
Who's there?
Kim.
Kim who?
Kim too late for the party.

Knock-knock!
Who's there?
Olive.
Olive who?
Olive here, let me in!

Knock-knock!
Who's there?
Imus.
Imus who?
Imus be outta my mind.

KNOCK-NAMES

Knock-knock!
Who's there?
Sarah.
Sarah who?
Sarah echo in here?

Knock-knock!
Who's there?
Albie.
Albie who?
Albie glad when you finally let me in.

Knock-knock!
Who's there?
Gladys.
Gladys who?
Gladys not snowing.

KNOCK-NAMES

Knock-knock!
Who's there?
Ida.
Ida who?
Ida know...sorry.

Knock-knock!
Who's there?
Darren.
Darren who?
Darren you to open the door.

Knock-knock!
Who's there?
Wynn.
Wynn who?
Wynn a few, lose a few.

KNOCK-NAMES

Knock-knock!
Who's there?
Claire.
Claire who?
Claire the way! I'm comin' through.

Knock-knock!
Who's there?
Tyrone.
Tyrone who?
Tyrone shoelaces.

Knock-knock!
Who's there?
Isabel.
Isabel who?
Isabel ringing or am I going nuts?

KNOCK-NAMES

Knock-knock!
Who's there?
Anita.
Anita who?
Anita use the toilet.

Knock-knock!
Who's there?
Nadya.
Nadya who?
**Nadya head if you understand
this joke.**

Knock-knock!
Who's there?
Byron.
Byron who?
Byron, get one free.

13

Doc-Doc!

Who's there?

Esther.

Esther who?

Esther a doctor in the house?

Doc-Doc!

Who's there?

Czar.

Czar who?

Czar a different doctor in the house?

Doc-Doc!

Who's there?

Gargoyle.

Gargoyle who?

**Gargoyle with salt water for
a sore throat.**

Doc-Doc!

Who's there?

Watts.

Watts who?

Watts up, Doc?

DOC KNOCKS

Doc-Doc!
Who's there?
Venice.
Venice who?
Venice the last time you saw a doctor?

Doc-Doc!
Who's there?
Colin.
Colin who?
Colin the doctor, of course.

Doc-Doc!
Who's there?
A knock-knock joke with a cold.

Doc-Doc!
Who's there?
Otto.
Otto who?
Otto know, who are you?

Doc-Doc!
Who's there?
Denise.
Denise who?
Denise are above de ankles.

Doc-Doc!
Who's there?
Schick.
Schick who?
Schick as a dog.

DOC KNOCKS

Doc-Doc!
Who's there?
Genoa.
Genoa who?
Genoa good dentist?

Doc-Doc!
Who's there?
Vicki.
Vicki who?
Vicki to good health is a healthy diet.

Doc-Doc!
Who's there?
Henrietta.
Henrietta who?
Henrietta worm that was in his apple.

DOC KNOCKS

Doc-Doc!
Who's there?
Dublin.
Dublin who?
Dublin over in pain from all these knock-knock jokes.

Doc-Doc!
Who's there?
Mia.
Mia who?
Mia stomach is killing me from laughing.

Doc-Doc!
Who's there?
Kenya.
Kenya who?
Kenya call the doctor, please?

Doc-Doc!
Who's there?
Goliath.
Goliath who?
Goliath down, you look sick.

Doc-Doc!
Who's there?
Dispense.
Dispense who?
**Dispense are too tight.
I must have gained weight.**

Doc-Doc!
Who's there?
Iota.
Iota who?
Iota send you to the hospital.

DOC KNOCKS

Doc-Doc!

Who's there?

Disease.

Disease who?

Disease the worst disaster I've ever seen.

Doc-Doc!

Who's there?

Morrie.

Morrie who?

**Morrie tells knock-knock jokes,
the sicker I feel.**

Doc-Doc!

Who's there?

Eileen.

Eileen who?

**Eileen on a crutch because I broke
my foot.**

DOC KNOCKS

Doc-Doc!
Who's there?
Concha.
Concha who?
Concha get rid of these chicken pox?

Doc-Doc!
Who's there?
Hatch.
Hatch who?
I'll come back when you stop sneezing.

Doc-Doc!
Who's there?
Oldest.
Oldest who?
**Oldest knocking has bruised
my knuckles.**

Doc-Doc!

Who's there?

Goose.

Goose who?

Goose see a doctor for that cough.

Doc-Doc!

Who's there?

Ada.

Ada who?

Ada whole box of chocolates and now I'm sick.

Doc-Doc!

Who's there?

Issue.

Issue who?

Issue the doctor?

DOC KNOCKS

Doc-Doc!
Who's there?
Althea.
Althea who?
Althea next time.

Doc-Doc!
Who's there?
Nita.
Nita who?
**Nita cure for all these
knock-knock jokes.**

Doc-Doc!
Who's there?
Moose.
Moose who?
Moose have been something I ate.

DOC KNOCKS

Doc-Doc!
Who's there?
Viper.
Viper who?
Viper nose, it's running.

Knock-knock!
Who's there?
Aiken.
Aiken who?
Oh, my Aiken back.

Doc-Doc!
Who's there?
Moustache.
Moustache who?
Moustache you to stop telling knock-knock jokes.

14

Knock-knock!

Who's there?

Yah.

Yah who?

Ride 'em, cowboy!

KNOCK 'EM COWBOY!

Knock-knock!
Who's there?
Tick.
Tick who?
Tick 'em up! This is a robbery.

Knock-knock!
Who's there?
Despair.
Despair who?
Despair of cowboy boots is too tight.

Knock-knock!
Who's there?
Orange.
Orange who?
Orange you Billy the Kid?

KNOCK 'EM COWBOY!

Knock-knock!
Who's there?
Cattle.
Cattle who?
Cattle purr if you pet her.

Knock-knock!
Who's there?
July.
July who?
July awake at night counting sheep?

Knock-knock!
Who's there?
Pasture.
Pasture who?
Pasture bedtime, cowpoke!

KNOCK 'EM COWBOY!

Knock-knock!
Who's there?
Beecher.
Beecher who?
Beecher to the draw again.

Knock-knock!
Who's there?
Dewey.
Dewey who?
Dewey have any more beef jerky?

Knock-knock!
Who's there?
Alma Gibbons.
Alma Gibbons who?
**Alma Gibbons you twenty-four hours
to get out of town.**

KNOCK 'EM COWBOY!

Knock-knock!
Who's there?
Mustang.
Mustang who?
Mustang up the phone. Chow's on.

Knock-knock!
Who's there?
Event.
Event who?
Event thataway!

Knock-knock!
Who's there?
Russell.
Russell who?
Russell up some grub!

KNOCK 'EM COWBOY!

Knock-knock!
Who's there?
Mike Howe.
Mike Howe who?
Mike Howe is sick. Gotta call the vet.

Knock-knock!
Who's there?
Lass.
Lass who?
Lass-o that cow if you can.

Knock-knock!
Who's there?
Orson.
Orson who?
Orson around again?

KNOCK 'EM COWBOY!

Knock-knock!
Who's there?
Agate.
Agate who?
Agate you covered, outlaw!

Knock-knock!
Who's there?
Icon.
Icon who?
Icon hardly wait to get back to my bunk.

Knock-knock!
Who's there?
Sonya.
Sonya who?
Sonya foot? I can smell it from here.

KNOCK 'EM COWBOY!

Knock-knock!
Who's there?
Danged Bob Dwyer.
Danged Bob Dwyer who?
**Danged Bob Dwyer ripped
my pants again.**

Knock-knock!
Who's there?
Gideon.
Gideon who?
Gideon your horse and giddyup.

Knock-knock!
Who's there?
Calder.
Calder who?
Calder sheriff! I've been robbed.

Knock-knock!
Who's there?
Owl.
Owl who?
Owl aboard, the train is leaving.

Knock-knock!
Who's there?
European.
European who?
European all over my favorite boots.

Knock-knock!
Who's there?
Barbara.
Barbara who?
Barbara black sheep, have you any wool?

KNOCK 'EM COWBOY!

Knock-knock!
Who's there?
Yah.
Yah who?
I'm glad to see you too, pardner.

Knock-knock!
Who's there?
Robin.
Robin who?
Robin banks is no way to make a living.

Knock-knock!
Who's there?
Sawyer.
Sawyer who?
Sawyer picture on a wanted poster.

Knock-knock!
Who's there?
Arizona.
Arizona who?
Arizona room for one of us in this town.

Knock-knock!
Who's there?
Manuel.
Manuel who?
**Manuel be sorry if you don't open
this door!**

Knock-knock!
Who's there?
Cod.
Cod who?
Cod you red-handed with the loot!

163

15

WHO'S KNOCKING?

Knock-knock!

Who's there?

Yah.

Yah who?

No thanks, I prefer Google.

Knock-knock!
Who's there?
Abe Lincoln.
Abe Lincoln who?
**Wait! You don't know who
Abe Lincoln is?**

Knock-knock!
Who's there?
Omelet.
Omelet who?
Omelet smarter than you think!

Knock-knock!
Who's there?
Canoe.
Canoe who?
Canoe loan me $20?

Knock-knock!
Who's there?
Dozen.
Dozen who?
Dozen anybody know how to answer a door?

Knock-knock!
Who's there?
Rover.
Rover who?
It's all Rover between us.

Knock-knock!
Who's there?
Bitter.
Bitter who?
Bitter watch your step.

WHO'S KNOCKING?

Knock-knock!
Who's there?
Fido.
Fido who?
Fido I always have to knock?

Knock-knock!
Who's there?
Midas.
Midas who?
Midas well open up.

Knock-knock!
Who's there?
Wooden shoe.
Wooden shoe who?
Wooden shoe like to know!

WHO'S KNOCKING?

Knock-knock!
Who's there?
Eva.
Eva who?
Eva told you, would you let me in?

Knock-knock!
Who's there?
Acid.
Acid who?
Acid let me in!

Knock-knock!
Who's there?
Huron.
Huron who?
Huron on my foot!

WHO'S KNOCKING?

Knock-knock!
Who's there?
Turnip.
Turnip who?
Turnip the heat, it's freezing in here!

Knock-knock!
Who's there?
Boise.
Boise who?
Boise a sore loser!

Knock-knock!
Who's there?
Jamaica.
Jamaica who?
Jamaica me a chocolate cake?

WHO'S KNOCKING?

Knock-knock!
Who's there?
Pencil.
Pencil who?
Your pencil fall down with no belt.

Knock-knock!
Who's there?
Ether.
Ether who?
Ether Bunny.

Knock-knock!
Who's there?
Samoa.
Samoa who?
Samoa Ether Bunnies.

WHO'S KNOCKING?

Knock-knock!
Who's there?
Toad.
Toad who?
Toad you before but you forgot.

Knock-knock!
Who's there?
Lass.
Lass who?
Lass one in is a rotten egg.

Knock-knock!
Who's there?
Irish.
Irish who?
Irish you a merry Christmas and a happy New Year.

Knock-knock!
Who's there?
Bacon.
Bacon who?
I'm bacon a cake for your birthday.

Knock-knock!
Who's there?
Ach.
Ach who?
Gesundheit!

Knock-knock!
Who's there?
Chicken.
Chicken who?
Chicken to see if you're awake.

WHO'S KNOCKING?

Knock-knock!
Who's there?
Ferry.
Ferry who?
Ferry funny, now let me in!

Knock-knock!
Who's there?
Willa.
Willa who?
Willa stop it with the corny knock-knock jokes?

Knock-knock!
Who's there?
Juicy.
Juicy who?
Juicy anyone else out here?

WHO'S KNOCKING?

Knock-knock!
Who's there?
Shoes.
Shoes who?
Shoes me. Can I be excused?

Knock-knock!
Who's there?
Major.
Major who?
Major ask, didn't I?

Knock-knock!
Who's there?
Vilify.
Vilify who?
Vilify knew my name, I would tell you.

WHO'S KNOCKING?

Knock-knock!
Who's there?
Zagat.
Zagat who?
Zagat in the Hat!

Knock-knock!
Who's there?
Goldilocks.
Goldilocks who?
Goldilocks herself out of the house all the time.

Knock-knock!
Who's there?
Papaya.
Papaya who?
Papaya the sailor man.

16

KNEE KNOCKS

Knock-knock!

Who's there?

Yeti.

Yeti who?

Yeti 'nother knock-knock joke.

Knock-knock!
Who's there?
Yule.
Yule who?
Open this door or yule be sorry.

Knock-knock!
Who's there?
Howl.
Howl who?
**Howl you know unless you open
the door?**

Knock-knock!
Who's there?
Hugo.
Hugo who?
Hugo first, I'm scared.

KNEE KNOCKS

Knock-knock!
Who's there?
Freda.
Freda who?
Freda letting me in, aren't you?

Knock-knock!
Who's there?
Fangs.
Fangs who?
Fangs for opening the door.
Bwah-ha-ha!

Knock-knock!
Who's there?
Jess.
Jess who?
Jess me and my shadow.

Knock-knock!
Who's there?
Barry.
Barry who?
Barry my bones in the graveyard.

Knock-knock!
Who's there?
Thumping.
Thumping who?
Thumping green and thlimy ith crawling up your leg!

Knock-knock!
Who's there?
Leaf.
Leaf who?
Leaf me alone!

Knock-knock!
Who's there?
Wash out.
Wash out who?
Wash out for the zombies!

Knock-knock!
Who's there?
Ivor.
Ivor who?
Ivor let me in or I'll blow your house down.

Knock-knock!
Who's there?
Gruesome.
Gruesome who?
Gruesome much my clothes don't fit.

Knock-knock!
Who's there?
Mustard bean.
Mustard bean who?
Mustard bean a surprise to find Bigfoot at your door.

Knock-knock!
Who's there?
Ice cream.
Ice cream who?
Ice cream every time I see your face.

Knock-knock!
Who's there?
Witches.
Witches who?
Witches the way home?

Knock-knock!
Who's there?
Hoosier.
Hoosier who?
Hoosier 'fraid of the Big Bad Wolf?

Knock-knock!
Who's there?
Flea.
Flea who?
Flea while you can!

Knock-knock!
Who's there?
Cinnamon.
Cinnamon who?
Cinnamonster, bolt the door!

Knock-knock!
Who's there?
Ding-dong.
Ding-dong who?
"Ding-dong, the witch is dead."

Knock-knock!
Who's there?
Ooze.
Ooze who?
Ooze going to open the door?

Knock-knock!
Who's there?
Diesel.
Diesel who?
Diesel be your last chance to let me in!

KNEE KNOCKS

Knock-knock!
Who's there?
Philip.
Philip who?
Philip this bag with treats, please.

Knock-knock!
Who's there?
Donatello.
Donatello who?
Donatello anyone—I'm a werewolf.

Knock-knock!
Who's there?
Keith.
Keith who?
Keith me! I want to be a prince again.

KNEE KNOCKS

Knock-knock!
Who's there?
Ivan.
Ivan who?
Ivan to drink your blood.

Knock-knock!
Who's there?
Deluxe.
Deluxe who?
Deluxe Ness Monster.

Knock-knock!
Who's there?
Lucretia.
Lucretia who?
Lucretia from the Black Lagoon.

KNEE KNOCKS

Knock-knock!
Who's there?
Frank N.
Frank N. who?
Frank N. Stein.

Knock-knock!
Who's there?
Hallways.
Hallways who?
Hallways knew you were a vampire.

Knock-knock!
Who's there?
Mohair.
Mohair who?
**There's mohair on your wart than
on your head.**

KNEE KNOCKS

Knock-knock!
Who's there?
Dutch.
Dutch who?
Dutch me and I'll scream!

Knock-knock!
Who's there?
Spell.
Spell who?
W-H-O.

Knock-knock!
Who's there?
Aida.
Aida who?
Aida whole village and now I'm gonna eat you.

Knock-knock!
Who's there?
Icy.
Icy who?
Icy a monster under your bed.

Knock-knock!
Who's there?
Sadie.
Sadie who?
Sadie magic word and I'll let you in.

Knock-knock!
Who's there?
Needle.
Needle who?
Needle little help getting away from Godzilla.

Knock-knock!
Who's there?
Vino.
Vino who?
Vino how to make you talk.

Knock-knock!
Who's there?
Crypt.
Crypt who?
Crypt up behind you!

Knock-knock!
Who's there?
Voodoo.
Voodoo who?
Voodoo you think you are?

17

KNOCK AROUND THE HOUSE

Knock-knock!

Who's there?

Norma Lee.

Norma Lee who?

Norma Lee I'd ring the doorbell.

Knock-knock!

Who's there?

Chicken.

Chicken who?

**Chicken your pocket.
I think your key's in there.**

Knock-knock!

Who's there?

Pasta.

Pasta who?

Pasta bread, I'm hungry.

Knock-knock!

Who's there?

Arthur.

Arthur who?

Arthur any brownies left?

KNOCK AROUND THE HOUSE

Knock-knock!
Who's there?
Bean.
Bean who?
Bean a long time since breakfast.

Knock-knock!
Who's there?
Eyewash.
Eyewash who?
Eyewash the dishes, you dry.

Knock-knock!
Who's there?
Alma.
Alma who?
Alma cookies are gone!

Knock-knock!
Who's there?
Dwayne.
Dwayne who?
Dwayne the bathtub, I'm dwowning.

Knock-knock!
Who's there?
Ammonia.
Ammonia who?
Ammonia a little kid. Let me in!

Knock-knock!
Who's there?
House.
House who?
House about opening this door?

Knock-knock!
Who's there?
Lego.
Lego who?
Lego of the door handle!

Knock-knock!
Who's there?
Dishes.
Dishes who?
Dishes me, silly!

Knock-knock!
Who's there?
Butternut.
Butternut who?
Butternut go outside, it's raining.

Knock-knock!
Who's there?
Tuba.
Tuba who?
Tuba toothpaste.

Knock-knock!
Who's there?
Megan.
Megan who?
Megan apple pie for dessert.

Knock-knock!
Who's there?
Ivana.
Ivana who?
Ivana go to Disneyland.

Knock-knock!
Who's there?
Pizza.
Pizza who?
Pizza chocolate cake would be good.

Knock-knock!
Who's there?
Dismay.
Dismay who?
Dismay be the last time I come to *your* house.

Knock-knock!
Who's there?
Needle.
Needle who?
Needle little snack.

Knock-knock!
Who's there?
Hominy.
Hominy who?
Hominy times do I have to knock?

Knock-knock!
Who's there?
Window.
Window who?
Window we get to play something else?

Knock-knock!
Who's there?
Psalm.
Psalm who?
Psalm day I'm going to get
my own room.

Knock-knock!

Who's there?

Beets.

Beets who?

Beets me, I can't even remember my name.

Knock-knock!

Who's there?

Alcott.

Alcott who?

Alcott the cake, you pour the milk.

Knock-knock!

Who's there?

Peas.

Peas who?

Peas pass the milk.

Knock-knock!
Who's there?
Belladonna.
Belladonna who?
Belladonna work so I had to knock.

Knock-knock!
Who's there?
Eton.
Eton who?
Eton out of the garbage is gross!

Knock-knock!
Who's there?
Cash.
Cash who?
No thanks, I'm allergic to nuts.

KNOCK AROUND THE HOUSE

Knock-knock!
Who's there?
Goat.
Goat who?
Goat to your room right now!

Knock-knock!
Who's there?
Hewlett.
Hewlett who?
Hewlett the dogs out?

Knock-knock!
Who's there?
Egg roll.
Egg roll who?
Egg roll off the table and broke.

Knock-knock!
Who's there?
Sausage.
Sausage who?
I never sausage a mess!

Knock-knock!
Who's there?
Dryer.
Dryer who?
Dryer you trying to get into my house?

Knock-knock!
Who's there?
Justice.
Justice who?
Justice I suspected—you stole the pie!

Knock-knock!
Who's there?
Emmett.
Emmett who?
Emmett the back door, not the front.

Knock-knock!
Who's there?
Queen.
Queen who?
Queen up your room.

Knock-knock!
Who's there?
Clothesline.
Clothesline who?
**Clothesline all over the floor.
What a mess!**

18

CAMP KNOCK-KNOCK

Knock-knock!

Who's there?

Intense.

Intense who?

Intense is where scouts sleep.

Knock-knock!
Who's there?
Scott.
Scott who?
Scott to be bears in these woods.

Knock-knock!
Who's there?
Gnats.
Gnats who?
Gnats the way the cookie crumbles.

Knock-knock!
Who's there?
Beehive.
Beehive who?
Beehive yourself or else!

Knock-knock!
Who's there?
Cook.
Cook who?
Yes. Yes, you are.

Knock-knock!
Who's there?
Itch.
Itch who?
Itch a long way to camp.

Knock-knock!
Who's there?
Donalette.
Donalette who?
Donalette the bedbugs bite.

Knock-knock!

Who's there?

Spider.

Spider who?

In spider everything, you're my best friend.

Knock-knock!

Who's there?

Bee.

Bee who?

Bee nice and build a fire.

Knock-knock!

Who's there?

Esther.

Esther who?

Esther a scorpion in your sleeping bag?

CAMP KNOCK-KNOCK

Knock-knock!
Who's there?
Roach.
Roach who?
Roach you a letter from camp.

Knock-knock!
Who's there?
Antson.
Antson who?
Antson my pants make me do a dance.

Knock-knock!
Who's there?
A pile-up.
A pile-up who?
A pile-up poo attracts flies.

Knock-knock!
Who's there?
Edward B.
Edward B. who?
Edward B. nice if you cleaned the cabin.

Knock-knock!
Who's there?
Zombies.
Zombies who?
Zombies just flew in the tent.

Knock-knock!
Who's there?
Wren.
Wren who?
Wren it rains, it pours.

CAMP KNOCK-KNOCK

Knock-knock!
Who's there?
Oliver.
Oliver who?
Oliver clothes got soaked in the rain.

Knock-knock!
Who's there?
Water.
Water who?
Water you doing up after lights out?

Knock-knock!
Who's there?
Achilles.
Achilles who?
**Achilles mosquitoes
if they don't stop biting me.**

Knock-knock!
Who's there?
Sparrow.
Sparrow who?
Sparrow me the details.

Knock-knock!
Who's there?
Ken.
Ken who?
Ken you hear something growling?

Knock-knock!
Who's there?
Quack.
Quack who?
Quack another joke and I'm outta here.

CAMP KNOCK-KNOCK

Knock-knock!
Who's there?
Dawn.
Dawn who?
Dawn wake me up so early.

Knock-knock!
Who's there?
Toucan.
Toucan who?
Toucan play this game.

Knock-knock!
Who's there?
Arthur.
Arthur who?
Arthur any snakes in this tent?

Knock-knock!
Who's there?
Wire.
Wire who?
Wire you eating that bug?

Knock-knock!
Who's there?
Hive.
Hive who?
Hive been workin' on the railroad.

Knock-knock!
Who's there?
Jethro.
Jethro who?
Jethro, ro, ro your boat...

CAMP KNOCK-KNOCK

Knock-knock!
Who's there?
Butternut.
Butternut who?
Butternut snore too loud.

Knock-knock!
Who's there?
Bat.
Bat who?
Bat you can't guess!

Knock-knock!
Who's there?
Hawk.
Hawk who?
Hawk...who goes there?

Knock-knock!

Who's there?

Romeo.

Romeo who?

Romeover to the other side of the lake and I'll tell you.

Knock-knock!

Who's there?

Spain.

Spain who?

Spain to be bitten by a horsefly.

Knock-knock!

Who's there?

Formosa.

Formosa who?

Formosa my life I've been allergic to bees.

214

Knock-knock!
Who's there?
Argo.
Argo who?
Argo fly a kite!

Knock-knock!
Who's there?
Bug spray.
Bug spray who?
Bug spray they won't get squished.

Knock-knock!
Who's there?
Mint.
Mint who?
**Mint to tell you about that
hornet's nest.**

Knock-knock!
Who's there?
Oily.
Oily who?
The oily bird catches the worm.

Knock-knock!
Who's there?
Weevil.
Weevil who?
Weevil go swimming today.

Knock-knock!
Who's there?
Luke.
Luke who?
Luke out for snapping turtles in the lake.

Knock-knock!
Who's there?
Amy.
Amy who?
Amy-fraid of ghost stories.

Knock-knock!
Who's there?
Outer.
Outer who?
Outer my way, I'm comin' in!

Knock-knock!
Who's there?
Owls.
Owls who?
Owls well that ends well.

19

WILDER-KNOCKS

Knock-knock!

Who's there?

Detour.

Detour who?

Detour of de zoo starts in five minutes.

Knock-knock!
Who's there?
Weasel.
Weasel who?
Weasel while you work.

Knock-knock!
Who's there?
Oink oink.
Oink oink who?
Wow, a pig and owl at the door!

Knock-knock!
Who's there?
Walrus.
Walrus who?
**Walrus asking silly questions,
aren't you?**

WILDER-KNOCKS

Knock-knock!
Who's there?
Goat.
Goat who?
Goat to the door and find out.

Knock-knock!
Who's there?
Noah.
Noah who?
Noah guy with an ark? It's raining cats and dogs out here.

Knock-knock!
Who's there?
Anteater.
Anteater who?
Anteater dinner, but uncle didn't eat a thing.

Knock-knock!
Who's there?
Aurora.
Aurora who?
Aurora's coming from those bushes.

Knock-knock!
Who's there?
Celia.
Celia who?
Celia later, alligator.

Knock-knock!
Who's there?
Rhino.
Rhino who?
Rhino more knock-knock jokes
than you do.

WILDER-KNOCKS

Knock-knock!
Who's there?
Wet.
Wet who?
Wet me in, it's raining.

Knock-knock!
Who's there?
Thistle.
Thistle who?
Thistle make you laugh.

Knock-knock!
Who's there?
Catsup.
Catsup who?
Catsup a tree! Call the fire department.

Knock-knock!
Who's there?
Lionel.
Lionel who?
Lionel eat you if you get too close.

Knock-knock!
Who's there?
Rook.
Rook who?
Rook out! The sky is falling.

Knock-knock!
Who's there?
Ellie Fence.
Ellie Fence who?
Ellie Fence love peanuts.

Knock-knock!
Who's there?
Viaduct.
Viaduct who?
Who knows viaduct quacks?

Knock-knock!
Who's there?
Iguana.
Iguana who?
Iguana hold your hand!

Knock-knock!
Who's there?
Arf.
Arf who?
Arf forgot.

Knock-knock!
Who's there?
Foreign.
Foreign who?
Foreign 20 blackbirds baked in a pie.

Knock-knock!
Who's there?
Raisin.
Raisin who?
Raisin chickens is hard work.

Knock-knock!
Who's there?
Howl.
Howl who?
Howl we get away from all these knock-knock jokes?

WILDER-KNOCKS

Knock-knock!
Who's there?
Zookeeper.
Zookeeper who?
Zookeeper away from me.

Knock-knock!
Who's there?
Hewlett.
Hewlett who?
Hewlett the monkeys out of the cage?

Knock-knock!
Who's there?
Wendy Katz.
Wendy Katz who?
Wendy Katz away, de mice will play.

Knock-knock!
Who's there?
Forest.
Forest who?
Forest the number after three.

Knock-knock!
Who's there?
Detail.
Detail who?
Detail is wagging de dog.

Knock-knock!
Who's there?
Wes Q.
Wes Q. who?
Wes Q. me from the quicksand!

WILDER-KNOCKS

Knock-knock!
Who's there?
Claws.
Claws who?
Claws the door!
There's a grizzly outside.

Knock-knock!
Who's there?
Hugh.
Hugh who?
Hugh can't stop a charging rhino.

Knock-knock!
Who's there?
Llama.
Llama who?
Llama so glad to see you.

20

SCHOOL OF KNOCK-KNOCKS

Knock-knock!

Who's there?

Phineas.

Phineas who?

Phineas thing happened at school today.

Knock-knock!
Who's there?
Sid.
Sid who?
Sid down and get to work!

Knock-knock!
Who's there?
Radio.
Radio who?
Radio not, here I come!

Knock-knock!
Who's there?
Broken pencil.
Broken pencil who?
Forget it. This joke is pointless.

Knock-knock!

Who's there?

Earl.

Earl who?

Earl be glad when it's summer vacation.

Knock-knock!

Who's there?

Zizi.

Zizi who?

Zizi to pass the test when you study.

Knock-knock!

Who's there?

Dishwasher.

Dishwasher who?

**Dishwasher last chance.
Go see the principal!**

Knock-knock!

Who's there?

Jewel.

Jewel who?

Jewel be glad to know I won the spelling bee.

Knock-knock!

Who's there?

Norway.

Norway who?

Norway am I gonna miss recess.

Knock-knock!

Who's there?

Viper.

Viper who?

Viper feet, you're tracking mud in the hall.

Knock-knock!
Who's there?
Avocado.
Avocado who?
Avocado cold so I'm staying home.

Knock-knock!
Who's there?
Tennis.
Tennis who?
Tennis three plus seven.

Knock-knock!
Who's there?
Oz.
Oz who?
Oz just about to answer that question.

Knock-knock!
Who's there?
Russian.
Russian who?
Russian around because I'm late for school.

Knock-knock!
Who's there?
Diesel.
Diesel who?
"Diesel man, he played one, he played knick-knack on a drum."

Knock-knock!
Who's there?
Auto.
Auto who?
Auto know the answer, but I forgot.

SCHOOL OF KNOCK-KNOCKS

Knock-knock!
Who's there?
Mister.
Mister who?
Mister school bus again.

Knock-knock!
Who's there?
Juneau.
Juneau who?
Juneau the words to
The Star-Spangled Banner?

Knock-knock!
Who's there?
Thermos.
Thermos who?
Thermos be some way out of doing
all this homework.

Knock-knock!
Who's there?
Babylon.
Babylon who?
Babylon if you want, but I'm not listening.

Knock-knock!
Who's there?
Repeat.
Repeat who?
Who! Who!

Knock-knock!
Who's there?
Pecan.
Pecan who?
Pecan someone your own size.

SCHOOL OF KNOCK-KNOCKS

Knock-knock!
Who's there?
F-2.
F-2 who?
Do I F-2 go to school today?

Knock-knock!
Who's there?
Swatter.
Swatter who?
Swatter you doing after school?

Knock-knock!
Who's there?
Danielle.
Danielle who?
Danielle at me, I didn't do anything.

Knock-knock!
Who's there?
Ahab.
Ahab who?
Ahab to go to the bathroom.

Knock-knock!
Who's there?
Censure.
Censure who?
Censure so smart, you do my homework.

Knock-knock!
Who's there?
Sam.
Sam who?
Sam old story. How about a new one?

Knock-knock!
Who's there?
Gladys.
Gladys who?
Gladys Friday!

Knock-knock!
Who's there?
Adam.
Adam who?
Adam up and tell me the total.

Knock-knock!
Who's there?
Sis.
Sis who?
Sis any way to treat your best friend?

Knock-knock!
Who's there?
Want.
Want who?
Good. Now try counting to three.

Knock-knock!
Who's there?
Giovanni.
Giovanni who?
Giovanni come out and play?

Knock-knock!
Who's there?
Festival.
Festival who?
Festival I have to finish my homework.

Knock-knock!
Who's there?
Chaos.
Chaos who?
Chaos the letter that comes after J.

Knock-knock!
Who's there?
Harris.
Harris who?
Harris your book report coming along?

Knock-knock!
Who's there?
Haiku.
Haiku who?
Haiku'd have danced all night!

21

KNOCK GOOD

Knock-knock!

Who's there?

Hair comb.

Hair comb who?

Hair comb the clowns.

KNOCK GOOD

Knock-knock!
Who's there?
I am.
I am who?
Oh, no! You forgot who you are?

Knock-knock!
Who's there?
Disguise.
Disguise who?
Disguise are where planes fly.

Knock-knock!
Who's there?
Pea.
Pea who?
Pea-u! Something stinks.

KNOCK GOOD

Knock-knock!
Who's there?
Darby.
Darby who?
Darby a lot of pirates in these waters.

Knock-knock!
Who's there?
Eve.
Eve who?
Eve-ho, me hearties!

Knock-knock!
Who's there?
Interrupting pirate.
Interrupting pirate wh—
Arrrrrh!

KNOCK GOOD

Knock-knock!
Who's there?
Water.
Water who?
Water you doing in my house?

Knock-knock!
Who's there?
France.
France who?
You know...France!
Where they make French fries.

Knock-knock!
Who's there?
Upton.
Upton who?
Upton no good...as usual.

KNOCK GOOD

Knock-knock!
Who's there?
Gumby.
Gumby who?
Gumby our guest for dinner.

Knock-knock!
Who's there?
Concha.
Concha who?
Concha come out and play?

Knock-knock!
Who's there?
Icing.
Icing who?
Icing off-key, so cover your ears.

KNOCK GOOD

Knock-knock!
Who's there?
Mikey.
Mikey who?
Mikey won't work, open the door!

Knock-knock!
Who's there?
Maida.
Maida who?
Maida Force be with you!

Knock-knock!
Who's there?
Yoda.
Yoda who?
Yoda one who won't open da door.

KNOCK GOOD

Knock-knock!
Who's there?
Howard.
Howard who?
Howard you like to be outside while somebody asks, "Who's there?"

Knock-knock!
Who's there?
Ashley.
Ashley who?
**Ashley, I changed my mind.
I don't want to come in.**

Knock-knock!
Who's there?
Turnip.
Turnip who?
Turnip the TV so I can hear it.

KNOCK GOOD

Knock-knock!
Who's there?
Winnie Thup.
Winnie Thup who?
And Tigger, too!

Knock-knock!
Who's there?
Mandy.
Mandy who?
Mandy lifeboats, we're sinking!

Knock-knock!
Who's there?
Butcher.
Butcher who?
Butcher right foot in, butcher right foot out...

KNOCK GOOD

Knock-knock!
Who's there?
Felix.
Felix who?
Felix my ice-cream cone again, he'll regret it.

Knock-knock!
Who's there?
Begonia.
Begonia who?
Begonia pardon, could you get off my foot?

Knock-knock!
Who's there?
Thumb.
Thumb who?
Thumb day my printh will come.

KNOCK GOOD

Knock-knock!
Who's there?
Wire.
Wire who?
Wire you drinking my hot chocolate?

Knock-knock!
Who's there?
Broccoli.
Broccoli who?
Don't be silly. Broccoli doesn't have a last name.

Knock-knock!
Who's there?
Letta.
Letta who?
Letta the dog outside.

Knock-knock!
Who's there?
Urine.
Urine who?
Urine so much trouble!

Knock-knock!
Who's there?
Muppet.
Muppet who?
Muppet up before somebody slips in it.

Knock-knock!
Who's there?
Xavier.
Xavier who?
Xavier breath.

KNOCK GOOD

Knock-knock!
Who's there?
Stopwatch.
Stopwatch who?
Stopwatch you're doing right now!

Knock-knock!
Who's there?
Utica.
Utica who?
Utica long way home today.

Knock-knock!
Who's there?
Foster.
Foster who?
Foster than a speeding bullet.

KNOCK GOOD

Knock-knock!
Who's there?
Erma.
Erma who?
"Erma little teapot, short and stout..."

Knock-knock!
Who's there?
Candy.
Candy who?
Candy knock-knock jokes stop now?

Knock-knock!
Who's there?
Dishes.
Dishes who?
Dishes the end of the book.